Slugs and snails.

snails

slugs

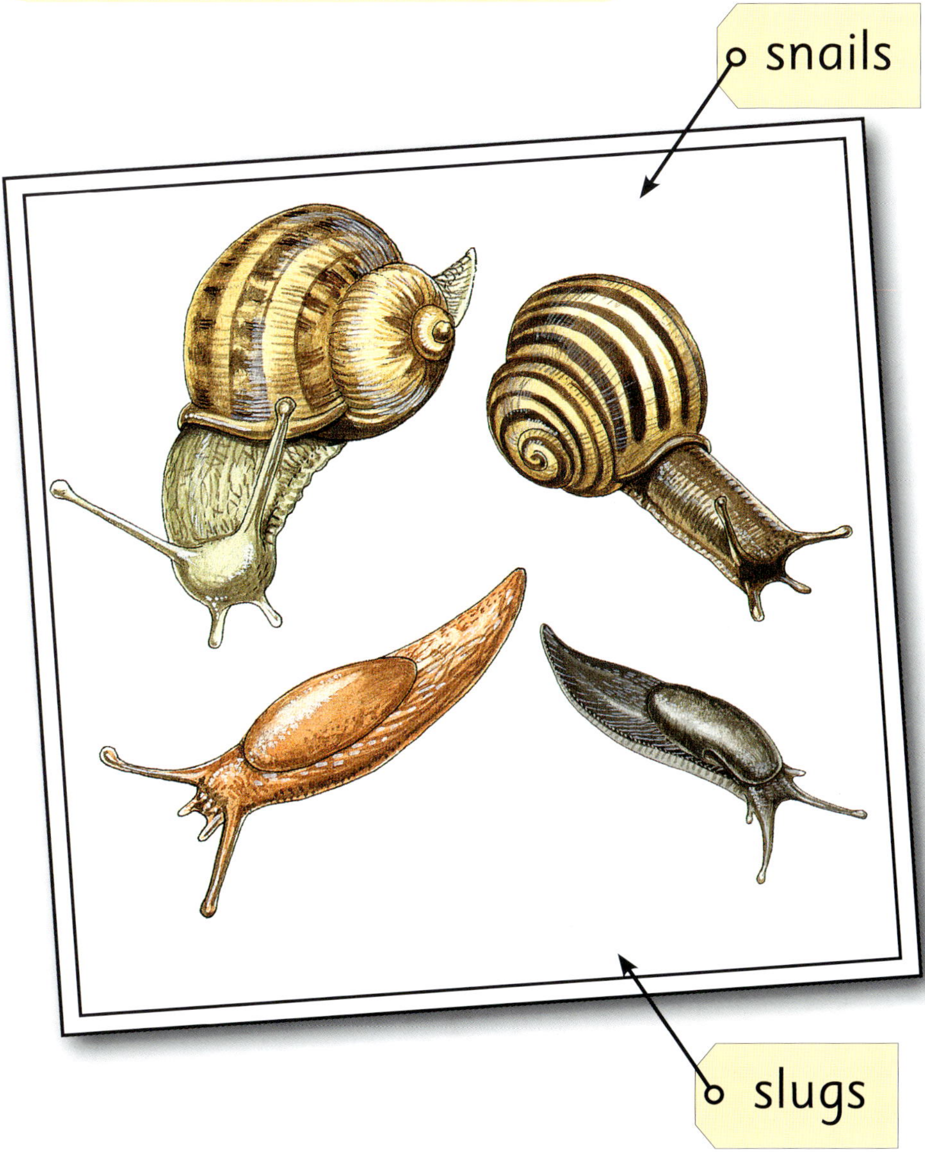

Snails have shells.

Slugs do not have shells.

As a snail gets bigger, its shell gets bigger too.

Slugs and snails hatch from eggs.

Slugs and snails live under things...

rock

...in the damp and dark.

This snail has left a silver trail on the ground.